'The eye of the mistress was wont to make her pew-
ter shine, and to inspect every part of her household furniture as much as her looking-glass.'
Addison 1716

THE SERVANTLESS HOUSEHOLD

HOW TO COPE - SOME POLITE ADVICE

Copper Beech Publishing

The Servantless Household

Published in Great Britain by
Copper Beech Publishing Ltd
This edition © Copper Beech Publishing Ltd 2002
Editor Jan Barnes

Originally printed in 1913 as part of 'First Aid to The Servantless'
With thanks to Blackwells UK for permission to reprint.

ISBN 1-898617-36-8
A CIP catalogue record for this book is available from The British Library.

Copper Beech Gift Books
Copper Beech Publishing Ltd
P O Box 159 East Grinstead
Sussex England RH19 4FS

CONTAINS:

WHO SHOULD BE SERVANTLESS?

Who ought to be servantless? It would be easier to name the people who should keep servants.

the wealthy The very wealthy, who are able to afford a retinue of high-trained, highly responsible domestics, and who advertise for a second housemaid of six or for a third footman of four. These owners of ample means must have servants just as they must have motor cars and pictures, caviar and pineapples.

At the other end of the social scale, come the working-mistresses, such as the lodging-house keepers, **busy tradesmen's wives** the busy tradesmen's wives, who assist in the shop. These women can keep in constant touch with their maid, they sit down to meals together with the maid, who becomes a member of the family.

For invalids, for lonely and timid spinsters, for helpless bachelors, the service of man and maid are not a matter of choice, but one of necessity.

helpless bachelors

> If only these solitary people of both sexes could be brought together and marry, we could eliminate one more class from those in need of servants!

Untidy persons who are always late, and always in a muddle, need a servant to help them out of their predicaments. So do lazy people, who cannot rise early and who are as handless as they are footless.

untidy

lazy people

Thus the rich house-holder, the striving working mistress, the solitary, the helpless, the thriftless and the shiftless must all depend on servants.
All other people might possibly be happier, healthier and wealthier if servantless.

CO-OPERATION

Early rising is essential for the servantless, method and order are indispensable.

The use of labour-saving implements is advisable, and above all co-operation is necessary; co-operation between the members of the family, between the house-holder and his tradesmen, and between acquaintances, friends and relations; also between the municipality and the house-holder.

Let this Machine do your
Washing Free.

LEISURE INTERVALS

Amongst the many objections raised by those who are advised to be servantless is that of the inexorable claim of domestic duties occupying all day and every day. Here, as elsewhere, the gift of condensing the labour must be cultivated. It will soon be acquired by practice, forethought and intelligence, and women of education have, or ought to have, powers of reflection and of understanding which no maid possesses.

How to find leisure intervals
To simplify the work without sacrificing the comfort, and thus creating leisure intervals, should be the aim of any servantless woman.

simplify

DRESS

How is one to dress when servantless? The answer is short and concise; dress with even greater neatness than before your maid departed. The idea that in order to do house work one must be in slatternly attire is a very false one, for the better one is dressed, the better one feels; but the dress must be an appropriate one.

appropriate

Freedom

short skirts

All good dressing means suitability to the occasion. The fashion of extremely short skirts is most favourable to the purpose. Not only does it allow freedom to flit quickly and to run upstairs, but also it prevents dust or fluff from being carried through the house.

In going up and down stairs it is a good plan always to pause and think if there is anything to carry and one rarely will have to move about empty handed.

The overall
The best plan is to have your dress covered entirely by a pretty but *substantial* overall. It should be made with very loose sleeves. All sleeves should be innocent of buttons or studs, for nothing is more destructive to furniture, mirrors and windowpanes than buttons or links carelessly drawn across polished surfaces, which thus become scratched as if by a cat! If your sleeves are already made with buttons and button holes, add a second hole where the button originally was and draw a ribbon through both - preferably a washable ribbon.

Many pockets

The overall should be provided with many pockets, one large one for the duster (which must always be handy and clean), others for the innumerable small things to carry about; things which the maid would have spent innumerable minutes in fetching and hunting for.

A housewife should also wear a kind of chatelaine such as hospital nurses wear, for scissors, knife, pin-cushion, a case for needles and pins, thimble and cotton, in order to put in easily the proverbial stitch in time. One of the pockets should hold a pencil and note book so as to make any memoranda or to write out instantly any orders to tradesmen. By thus carrying in the various pockets - some of which could be buttoned up - the implements likely to be constantly required needless steps will be saved and also much time economised.

The sun bonnet

Though in a servantless house, and especially in one where a vacuum machine is used, dust should be reduced to its minimum, some dust will be created during each day's work, and therefore a woman's hair must be protected.

Nothing is so good for that purpose and nothing is so becoming as a sun bonnet made of chintz or print. It will suit everyone, it will enhance the beauty of the young face and shade the defects of worn features. It could be made quite easily in a collapsible form and have a permanent home in one of the many pockets.

These numerous pockets of the overall may compensate for the pocketless gowns imposed on us by despotic dressmakers!

THE HANDS

The hands must be protected against dirt or roughness, and the fear of spoiling the hands forms a very important barrier to those who otherwise might be servantless. But if a hand is shapely and kept clean, no rough usage, neither gardening nor even masonry work, will injure it.

Only when the hand depends for beauty on coloured and well-manicured nails, must it have some protection.

Gloves
Nothing is better than the india-rubber gloves such as are worn by surgeons during operations. They entirely screen the hand, which can thus be ruthlessly placed in the hottest soda water, especially if

the hand is first powdered with fuller's earth and the glove at once drawn on. These gloves are so well made and so supple that they do not impede any movement, and they are comfortable to wear.

Dirty work
When very dirty work has to be done and a gloveless condition is imperative, fill the nails with soap, and then when cleaning the hands, use either vaseline or coarse brown sugar, before proceeding with the normal washing process.

Paper towels
Hands must be dried well or the skin will crack, and the best thing is to have in your overall pocket some paper towels. They are strong and absorbent, and come in handy in many other ways during the day's labours.

CARE OF THE FEET

The feet suffer much at first from unusual house work, partly because needless steps are taken and needless standing about is indulged in, and partly because the feet may not be suitably shod for the work.

The right shoes
High heels are most uncomfortable for the house-wife, and even may be injurious to her constitution, as they throw out the proper balance of the body. Neat, comfortable shoes, not too thin of sole, should be worn; and if the feet burn and ache at night a short immersion in water will refresh and insure sound sleep.

Long standing
When long standing has to be done, as for washing up or for ironing, it is wise to place a thick soft rug under the feet, such as a doubled up bath mat; a cork mat is also very comfortable if placed before the sink. It is warm and soft to the feet, and needs little cleaning.

a thick soft rug under the feet

Practice
To stand without fatigue is a matter of practice, and can be acquired. This skill has to be acquired by Royalties, Ambassadors and important hostesses; it means placing the feet in a proper position and well poising the body, for it is only slouchy standing on one foot which is so tiring.

17

THE FIGURE

Some think that the reason of the housemaid's contours being almost invariably better than her mistress's is because of the bed-making which accounts for the shapely form, but the maid rarely makes a bed; she simply covers it up; it is the constant movement that does it!

constant movement

Graceful as a bird
The maid, even if negligent, had to go about a great deal after all, had to race here, there and everywhere, up and down stairs and back again; thus movement became easy to her, and being perfectly easy, it is as graceful as that of a bird, and it often had been a pleasure to watch those swift motions.

SPARE ROOMS AND KITCHENS

As soon as the maid has driven off in her heavily-laden cab you become aware of the fact that there are several rooms in the house available now, which formerly were her exclusive property.

The maid's bedroom

There is of course the maid's bedroom, which when well scrubbed and aired and re-papered, will make a very nice spare room or a sewing room, or an extra bath or tubbing room.

several rooms in the home are free

The kitchen

How strange and how pleasant to feel that the kitchen now is the mistress's very own, and she can arrange it as she pleases; but it will also require cleaning, airing, whitewashing and distempering.

The pantry

Who will use the pantry when one is servantless? Surely it becomes immediately superfluous. Silver, glass and china are far better kept in the dining or living room to be taken out as required.

Where there are no wall-presses in the room a servantless housewife will be wise if she endeavours to buy a large cupboard or sideboard in which to store the fragile treasures; it should if possible also hold her table linen, while in the drawers silver and knives can be kept.

a large old-fashioned dresser The ideal piece of furniture is a large old-fashioned roomy dresser. By thus keeping everything in the living room, everything is at hand when setting or clearing the table; the washing-up of the dinner ware is best done on the large kitchen table, and the same tray that has brought the articles there will take them back to the sideboard.

Friends

Should a friend arrive suddenly to share a meal, all that has to be done is to take out the plates, knives and forks, glass and napkins, and there is no delay, no searching, no fussing or hunting; an extra place has merely to be set.

Slops

The subject of slops is one of the great bugbears of the owner of a servantless house. Slop pails and slop cloths ought to be removed to museums as being illustrative of the barbarous customs of primitive man! It seems inconceivable that refined people should allow such abominations to be carried about the house, generally proving obnoxious, to the danger of stair carpet.

refined people

Where there are many in a house who all want to tub, wash and dress at the same moment, only a few minutes can be allowed to each in the bathroom, but the moment the maid has departed everything changes and there are two extra places with hot and cold water taps available for ablution.

The scullery used as a bathroom

Consider the now almost useless scullery. Wash, bathe and dress in the scullery? but why not? there is nothing in a name, and a maidless scullery is merely a room like any other. It could be curtained off for warmth and seclusion, it is almost certain to possess a gas-burner - hence a gas stove can be readily adapted for heating purposes. The floor could be well covered with a cork carpet.

Sand under linoleum

By the by, on a stone floor which has probably worn unevenly, it is a good plan to spread a thick layer of very fine sifted sand before placing the cork carpet or linoleum. The sand will also absorb any underneath moisture created by the excessive water splashing and spilling of the average male bather.

Breakfast
Breakfast is best taken in the kitchen. The kitchen is the pleasantest part of a house at breakfast time. In its cosy corner, well screened from draughts, the dishes taken piping hot (or kept piping hot for sluggards) taste ever so much better. Preferably the breakfast table has been set overnight, covered all over with a large muslin. Porridge will have been made overnight. Coffee is also quite ready.

cosy corner

23

COOKERY

Where cooking is good, people have happy faces; they work cheerfully amid song and laughter. Where cooking is bad, faces are long and sad, and both work and play are taken gloomily.

Two kinds of cooking

the plain cook
Many volumes have been written about the British plain cook, but what is meant by plain cooking can be a mystery. There are only two kinds of cooking - good or bad!

Cookery as an art
Art can only be judged by results. The artist in cookery must possess a large number of combined qualities: the first is intelligence; forethought is needed, and cleanliness is imperative.

The fine palate

The good cook must have a fine palate, and unless that is possessed, all conscientious work is thrown away.

Accuracy

Most women cooks, instead of measuring, weighing and timing, trust to instinct, with the result of producing, - at least some of the time - an inferior and imperfect meal.

instinct

When a woman is a good cook she is certain to be an artist, taking time and trouble over her work, and being proud of it when it succeeds.

THE KITCHEN - PLANNING

Consider the ideal kitchen such as it could be built, or such as an existing one could be converted into.

First remove the kitchen range, and next remove the dresser. Replace the range either by a radiator, or by a gas cooking range with a gas open fire, or by an open fire place. The open fireplace is the prettiest and most comfortable, and if fitted with a grate and drawer it will burn for many hours unattended and will need hardly any cleaning.

The table
In place of the usual dresser have tables, shelves and brackets as follows:
In the first place, fix a table in the wall made with a large flap which should be fashioned of hard wood

such as beech and not of absorbent soft deal. The flap should be supported by strong folding legs. It should be kept spotlessly clean, and the best way to clean it is with cold water and coarse sand. The object of the table being a folding one is to allow easy cleaning underneath and to make room for the family breakfast table, for shriek as you may, the first meal should be taken in the kitchen. Two shelves should run right round the kitchen walls on which we place pretty lettered canisters, also salt and matchboxes.

family breakfast

Ladle bracket

On the right of the cooker, should be a ladle bracket for large spoons and forks, the steak tongs and the 'grip-all'. The gravy and grease fall in the hollow part of this ladle bracket and thus it saves the table, the floor, the stove and the dress.

Steak tongs

Steak tongs and grips are indispensable to a lady cooking. If the steak tongs are used, by placing the thumb and second finger into the appropriate holes, anything can be lifted without soiling the hands. The 'grip-all' is quite a recent invention and will grip all safely, such as a baking tin, and thus again save the hands from heat or soot.

The zinc-covered table

On the other side of the cooker have an ordinary sized table, 3ft x 2ft, covered with zinc for placing saucepans, kettles or dishes straight from the fire. The zinc takes no harm from the blackened saucepan or greasy pot, and it can be polished up in a minute with a rag dipped in paraffin or sand to look like silver, every mark disappearing instantly from the metal.

The walls

Many architects advise that a kitchen wall should be tiled from floor to ceiling, or to a high dado, but this is costly to carry out.

Cover the walls with a light washable paper down from the ceiling to four feet from the floor, then have a brass rail, with hooks on it, and on these hooks have a ringed curtain right down to the floor, the curtain to be made of pretty coloured coarse heavy canvas. This can periodically go to the laundry and always look fresh and clean.

curtained
dado

The open fire

If you choose to have an open fire it will need coal, and this is one of the very great difficulties of the servantless home. Fetching coal, breaking it up, filling up coal buckets, is certainly no pleasant task, and the sooner it is done, the better.

> Every kitchen should have a coal bin which will not allow coal to drop on the floor.

ashes and cinders

A good coal should give little ash, but it may give many cinders, and it is a shame to throw these away. The work of cinder-sifting can hardly be called an agreeable one though.

Sifting

It is possible to find a simple arrangement of sheet iron, light and portable, by means of which cinders could be sifted (even in a drawing-room) with no dust arising. The upper and lower traps are closed during sifting, then the lower one is opened to empty into a bucket. All those who possess even a small garden should keep their ashes, but these must not be mixed with kitchen rubbish.

French Cinder-sifter

The dustbin

A so-called dustbin - even one that is termed hygienic - is one of those abominations to be placed in a prehistoric museum as illustrating savagery, together with the slop pail and slop cloth.

The cosy corner

If the kitchen is arranged so as to have a fireplace and a cooker, divide the room into two parts: the cosy living part near the fireplace, and the working part near the cooker.

divide into
two parts

Where practicable the cosy corner should be near a window, for though winters are long, summers are often trying, and no one suffers more from the heat than the artist who has to cook. The cosy corner should be screened off from the rest by one of those useful wooden folding screens.

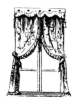

The fountain

An old fountain, or a good copy of an antique, is desirable in the kitchen: it can be made of wrought iron, of copper, or of crockery.

A good copy of an antique metal fountain lends a glow of colour to the kitchen and every woman will recognise the advantage of being able to wash her hands frequently and away from the sink and its splashing taps.

The cooker

If possible the cooker should be enamelled, for thus it will need merely to be dusted or wiped, and the horrible and useless ugly process of black-leading is avoided.

The height of the sink &c.

One of the great trials of housework is to have to either stoop too much, or to stand long on tip-toe. When the maid reigned supreme in the kitchen, the sink, the washing basins, the shelves, &c., were so as to suit the average stature but the housewife is probably as permanent as earthly conditions do allow, and if she is brave enough to be servantless, is worthy of the best possible setting.

Shelves

Too many implements are only in the way, but the necessary ones must be handy and hang round the walls, or be placed on convenient shelves. Needless running should be avoided. It is tiring, and something may spoil on the stove while you go to and fro.

Brackets

One idea is to have a saucepan-lid holder, graduated to size. Lids are always in the way, apt to tumble down with an irritating, rattling clatter. From another bracket should hang the necessary kitchen cloths - oven cloth, duster, glass cloth, each on their separate hook; from another bracket with hooks should hang all the kitchen knives.

Mops and brushes

From hooks should hang the various mops and brushes needed for cleaning.

The sink

If you are prepared to remain servantless, it is recommended that the sink should at once transfer to the kitchen itself. Mrs Beeton in her wonderful book shows the sink to be under the kitchen window, &c. No fear of smells or nuisances need arise; a sink can be kept as clean and as sweet as a rose bowl in the drawing room.

> There is a special kind of sink with a lid which can be fitted to cover it entirely, then a plant or flower-vase can be placed on it when the washing operations are not going on.

The clock
The clock must not be forgotten, nor must you omit a slate for memoranda; a board with pegs as a reminder of stores to be procured is also a great convenience. If expense has to be considered, this board could easily be home-made, and matches will do instead of pegs to place against: 'sugar' 'tea,' 'coffee,' &c.

the house-keeper's reminder

Paper
A useful tip is to have in various parts of the kitchen packets of soft paper neatly cut in convenient sizes, hanging readily accessible. This will save endless work and much laundry expense if a piece of paper can always be snatched quickly for a variety of purposes, either to wipe off some grease spilled, or to put underneath anything, or to wrap up anything in a hurry.

Coffee
A coffee grinder should hang on the wall; these are now made at very moderate cost, in a very compact way, with a glass underneath to receive the grounds, the upper jar serving to hold the roasted beans, and, being transparent, showing at once the quantity of coffee beans in reserve.

THE HOT WATER SUPPLY

If the clumsy wasteful kitchen-range with its erratic boiler has been replaced by an open fire-place, and if we cook on oil, gas or electric stove, where is the hot water to come from?

Hot water
Hot water must be had, and plenty of it, and no doubt it is an immense gain to a servantless house to have at all times hot water - really hot, not lukewarm. (The maid's water was never *really* hot, so in summer, just when a bath is most appreciated after, say a dusty walk, or a railway excursion, the range had not been lighted and there was never any hot water.)

really hot water

The copper

Nearly every small house possesses a washing boiler
- commonly called the 'copper'; this is very unlikely
to be used for boiling clothes in a servantless home,
and can therefore be utilised for providing clean
hot water; the smallest fire will keep the water boiling, a good hand-scoop will ladle it out.
To fill the copper have the cold water supply pipe
brought just over it by a tap, or use a piece of hose,
with an adapter to the sink-cock. At night, stoke
the grate of this boiler with coal dust or briquettes.

Where baths are needed of a morning, it may be
assumed that at least some members of the family
are robust and can bathe in cold water.

For others, a provision of almost boiling water to
add to their tub can be made without any appre-

ciable expense. First boil the water: procure from a wine merchant a big stone bottle known as a demijohn, and holding a gallon at least; heat it well with hot water. Then, after emptying the first heating water, fill it to the very brim with fast boiling water, place the jar on a cork mat, and cover it with a big cosy which you have made beforehand.

a stone bottle

If the stone jar is really full, leaving no air space, if your water at the time of the jar filling is really boiling, if your cosy really covers the jar, the water, even on the frostiest morning, will be so hot that you need a holder with which to touch the stone bottle.

even on the frostiest morning

Thermos jug for shaving water
For shaving water the same plan can be pursued in a miniature way; where expense has not to be considered a small thermos jug can be bought.

39

FIRES AND HEATING APPARATUS

This part of household work is one of the most important and arduous, and that the fear of having to attend to fires prevents many a mistress from becoming servantless.

The old-fashioned range
In the kitchen the importance of a fire cannot be denied, and the old-fashioned range will still be in use in the majority of homes; not because it is efficient or economical, but simply because it is there. The first trouble about a kitchen range is that it is found to be dirty. The maid was always late coming downstairs, and hardly ever cleaned out the stove properly; she lighted it as quickly as ever she could to warm her hands and to boil the kettle for her early tea.

The sweep

If when you lift up parts of the range you see it is thickly coated with soot, you must send for the sweep, and you much watch him to see that he really clears all away. If while you wait for him to finish, you have crushed plenty of coarse kitchen salt, you can strew it where the sweep has left black imprints, for salt combines with soot till the mass is perfectly clean to handle.

coarse kitchen salt

A wise housekeeper should always have a box of crushed salt close to every hearth in case of sooty accidents. It is as well to make a friend of the jolly worker, for it is advisable if servantless to see him frequently; where a kitchener burns all day, it would not be too much to have it swept once a fortnight; that system would be saving of fuel in the end.

Cleaning the kitchener

During the fortnight, it is recommended to have a thorough daily cleaning of the pipe by means of the flue brush. Lift up all the parts of the stove, sprinkle them with salt, and thoroughly dust them. The top of the oven should be attended to, and also the soot-well should be cleared. If this is done each morning a clear, smokeless fire will be the reward. There is one difficulty, for breakfast should be taken in the kitchen, and there is no time to do all the cleaning before breakfast. Follow this plan: cover the fire at night with slack and ashes, opening the range as much as possible, so that it may be still burning in the early morning. On first coming down close all doors of the stove and make a good draught in it, because your family likes to see a bright fire after bathing. If you have saved the corks from your bottles, or have procured cork shavings and allowed them to soak in a jar of paraffin, you can throw some in the grate, and all will blaze up. Then, after breakfast, either while you make the beds or walk out, or dust, allow the kitchen fire to go out entirely. Next when the range is cool, give it its daily cleaning, do the cinder-sifting and coal-filling, then relight your kitcheners. After that polish the boots and do other things which are disagreeable and dirty to handle.

The great wish of a housewife who has to do all this will probably be to possess a gas cooker - but objections arise: the initial cost, the current expense, the heating of water for the baths and household, and above all the difficulty of keeping the kitchen warm when one is not cooking.

Modern appliances of gas companies
The modern gas companies will allow you to pay by instalments, they will show you how to do a maximum of cooking with a minimum of gas consumption, they will provide you with a water heating apparatus connected with, or independent of, your cooker; and what is the best of all, they can furnish you with a combined gas heating and cooking range.

Do without new dresses and bonnets, do without a holiday trip, and save every penny possible, such a range is the one to have if servantless: a year of the maid's wages would repay it, and the comfort is indescribable.

In the bedrooms

The old-fashioned way of hardening by robing, undressing and sleeping in ice-cold rooms is gradually disappearing. But at the close of a happy but busy day the servantless housewife has to do much in the warm kitchen - clear away all dinner things, prepare all breakfast things, fill hot-water bottles, cover up the fire, &c.

After this it would be a great risk for her to run up to bed in an arctic room; for it is on her health the comfort of the whole household depends.

CLEANING

Next to cooking, nothing is so mismanaged in the ordinary household as cleaning. Why should things be left about the passages and stairs? Why should halls be littered with dust-pans, brooms, pails, rolled-up mats to trip over? Either an implement is used, or it is not used. When in use it is not in the way: when not in use it should be put **slovenly** by; no time is gained, no labour is saved, by that **habit** slovenly habit of leaving implements about.

A plan
This is a plan to clean a house effectively. First stand on the front doorsteps made of stone, badly **a hard** soiled by yesterday's mud, by the dripping of the **task** milkman's can, and by the kicks of the baker's hob- **ahead** nailed boots; a hard task is ahead!

In addition, if the weather is damp and the morning is raw, the only thing to do is to say to oneself "*Never mind*", and clean away with a brush and plenty of water; then polish the door brasses.

Cleaning the front door brasses
If you take the precaution of rubbing a very little vaseline over them, brasses will not tarnish for many days; twice a week should suffice.

Doorstep
In time, a front doorstep cleaning brigade may form in the style of the window-cleaning companies and we will escape the drudgery of doorstep cleaning. Whitening the steps is as hideous as it is useless; on bad days cover them with soft sand and thus avoid much of the dirt. Ask all friends, relations and tradesmen to clean their feet on the scraper.

Dusting shoes

In summer, before letting anyone in at the front door, make them dust their shoes with a long-handled mop made of wool. Much dust and dirt will thus remain outside, and it should be regarded as uncivilized to carry dirt of any kind into a house. If you reflect of what you carry in, you would soon get into the habit of using scraper, mat and mop.

The lobby

Now into the lobby, which is tiled; tiles too are very difficult to clean. If someone has spilt the oil from his bicycle lamp last night on the flags, the only way to deal with the oily mark is to make a paste of fuller's earth and turpentine, smear it on the stain and leave it there; repeat the process until all grease is absorbed.

cleaning off marks of oil

Polished floors

The hall will have a polished floor; all polished floors should be first cleaned with fine steel shavings. They are scattered over the floor and swept off with a good broom; then apply a little beeswax mixed with turpentine by means of a rough cloth and a covered broom; rub briskly - not heavily - it is a splendid exercise, and if done in rhythm it amounts to pleasure. To get a high finish on a floor it is necessary to pass a large soft dry flannel over it and this will then keep clean for a week or more, needing to be merely swept with a soft broom daily.

it amounts
to pleasure

Scrubbing white wood articles

In the kitchen scrub the white wood objects - table, tubs, bread and meat boards, with cold water (the colder the better) and sand. Then throw a little sawdust about and sweep the floor - never wet it -

but make it spotless by wiping it over with a cloth dripped in turpentine. A kitchen floor should not be slippery, so instead of applying beeswax use a little skimmed milk or sour milk for the final polish; and the linoleum will last for a life-time.

Wooden stair-rods

Brass stair-rods give a great deal of trouble. Wooden stair-rods are now to be had, which look much better and require no polishing; they can be had in a variety of coloured wood and in a variety of shapes.

Bed-making

It must be remembered that we spend much of our life in bed. If a bed is very large and close to the wall, it is advisable to procure wooden rails on hinges: they fold under the bed and when the bed has to be drawn out, the rails are extended and the heavy pieces glide on them easily. Their use saves the floor, the carpet, or the linoleum.

To remove the fluff under a bed a large mop of white wool should be kept specially for the purpose; it is dipped in turpentine and passed under the furniture to collect any thread or bits: the task of dusting the room is thus very light.

> Bed-making is an art which requires conscientious carrying out.

Dusters

A good-sized wash-leather and a soft duster are indispensable - preferably the duster should be made of butter-muslin, for that material dusts beautifully and washes out like a piece of lace, and dries in a moment. These dusters and leathers should be

buttermuslin

kept in the overall pocket to be used for polished surfaces, the duster for china, books, papers and ornaments.

Spring cleaning

If a housewife cleans well daily, no big cleaning is ever necessary. It is a barbarous idea to allow a place to get so dirty that a great upheaval is necessary!

The uses of glycerine

Glycerine is a useful household article, and it is cheap. If applied to window-panes it will keep them from steaming, and thus save mopping up the sills on cold mornings.

cleaning boots and shoes

Glycerine is also extremely good for boots and shoes, and keeps them in perfect condition.

The boot rest
Good advice is to keep a boot-rest in the hall, and one in every room occupied by man or boy, to prevent his bad habit of placing the foot on chairs or other furniture when he laces up his footgear.

The slipper box
It is a good idea to have near the front entrance a slipper box; very handsome ones can now be purchased in metal, but a handy husband could easily make one out of a grocer's box. Each person should keep their slippers there and never go about the house without first exchanging out-door footgear for his slippers. If there is much going to and fro from a garden, clogs should be used.

WASHING UP

 Washing up is one of the bugbears of a servantless home. Immediately after use, collect all dirty crockery and silver. Each article should then, before the grease sets, be wiped with soft paper.

How to buy crockery
Those who are within reach of shops can now buy crockery at such a low price that there can hardly be an excuse for not having a large quantity of things in order to allow for only one daily washing up.

one daily washing up
A good plan in places where annual fairs are held is to purchase enough crockery at the fair - pudding-basins, pie-dishes, &c. to last a twelvemonth or more; often you can pick up great bargains in that way.

Dirty plates

Many people object that dirty plates left about all day make a litter and are in the way. That need not be; they can be all stowed away neatly out of sight; a large tin trunk would not be bad for the purpose.

Getting everything ready

When you actually wash up, you must first get everything ready - plenty of boiling water in three tubs, all in a row, best on the large kitchen table. Where space is limited, jugs instead of bowls will do to wash silver and knives in.

Burning the greasy papers

Having scraped off all scraps from the ware and burnt the greasy papers in the grate; you now have handy two mops, a hard one for the first water, in which a few soap flakes may be whipped up.

Very hot water necessary

Now wash each piece, one at a time, in the boiling water, using the hard mop in the first, the soft one in the next, and just passing each article in the last water: keep each water really hot by adding to it from the kettle. If you have no rubber gloves, use steak tongs or two wooden spoons to fish out your articles, for it is absolutely necessary to wash at great heat.

Then just place each piece in a plate rack or on a tray, and don't wipe anything; no cloth is needed at all excepting for the silver, and even for that use one or more of the cleanly, convenient, and hygienic paper towels, which can at once be destroyed.

Paper towels to wipe silver
A cloth is never really clean; it has touched other things, it has been washed together with other things, and remember a spoon for instance is put inside each mouth.

A thorough washing-up once a day should suffice for the average household. Silver done in this fashion never needs what is usually called "cleaning" i.e. messing with a scratchy powder or paste which collects in the chased parts, and then rubbing bright either with the thumb (as butlers do) or with a dubious leather.

Silver should be washed daily in three hot waters, piece by piece - that is essential; if you do more than one piece at a time, each article does not come out boiling hot, and it is the heat that is the secret of the polish, as the butler's thumb knows.

heat is the secret

57

Glass and bone spoons for egg foods and acids
Spoons and forks which have touched vinegar, or
which have been used for eggs, can be first rubbed
with fine table salt. But where labour has to be
saved, it is advisable to eat eggs with bone or glass
spoons, and to have bone or glass forks and spoons
for pickles, salads, rhubarb, or other acids.

The sink

spotless

Care of the sink can be heavy on a servantless
woman who is fastidious. The sink should be spotless, but tea leaves and coffee grounds stain the
white enamel or the metal to such an extent that
long scrubbing and rubbing are necessary. Never
allow either tea leaves or coffee grounds to be
thrown down a drain. Keep two special jars or tins,
one for tea leaves, one for coffee grounds. Use an
infuser in the tea-pot; this can be allowed to dry in

a jar, and use the liquor for cleaning varnished paint, or to sponge black dresses.

It is well to dry coffee grounds, and the economically inclined may know that dried coffee grounds do instead of knife powder, and cost nothing. When done with, burn them, or put them on flower beds; they form a good fertilizer.

How to wash glass
Glass should be washed in hot water and then rinsed in cold: it should be allowed to dry without wiping; then before putting it by, polish with a very clean piece of butter muslin. Decanters are best cleaned with a mixture of crushed egg-shells, vinegar, tea leaves and water.

Washing up saucepans

The washing-up of saucepans, baking tins, &c., should be done exactly in the same way as that of the crockery. First of all, stoneware implements should be used as much as possible for cooking.

Inside very greasy pots and pans use a very little piece of soft soap, about a teaspoon to a gallon of water, and rinse immediately in two other hot waters, or first boil up the pot on the range with the soap, taking care to watch it, as soap is apt to 'run over' like milk.

Putting by cooking utensils

All cooking utensils should be dried after washing, either on the range, or in the sun. They should never be wiped with a cloth, or be put by with their lids on, or they will rust or mildew. They should, if possible, all hang in the warm and airy kitchen with their faces turned to the wall. If the outside of metal saucepans or kettles is rubbed very lightly with vaseline or margarine, they will not blacken when put on the smokiest fire.

Waste paper baskets

For servantless women it is advisable to keep one or two waste paper baskets in the kitchen and to line them with washable covers; then every small piece of paper or cardboard, or tin cover of a cork, or rag, old faded flowers, or shavings from a parcel &c. can instantly be disposed of. Once a day these baskets can be emptied and their contents burned. A great saving of trouble is effected by having many such receptacles.

LAUNDRY WORK

In a small household, the departure of the house-maid will be most felt on washing day, though she felted the flannels, shrunk the socks, tore the lace frills, gave you a cold dinner, and allowed you to be in a soapy vapour bath all day. You will miss her even though you had to help her by folding things for the jolting mangle.

the mangle

House cloths

Kitchen and pantry cloths, tea cloths, and dusters are dispensed with; a duster of butter muslin is washed so easily that you can do it while you wash your hands, hence it does not count. Slop cloths have gone to the prehistoric museum, so all that remains of house cloths is the knife cloth.

Nappe de Famille
Where economy has to be studied, and where there
are children, the use of a *nappe de famille* is recommended instead of the usual table cloth. It is a kind
of oilcloth made to resemble a damask table cloth,
and is to be had in a variety of patterns and sizes.
When the meal is finished it is washed over with a
sponge then rolled up on a stick and put by.

The table cloth
You can use a *nappe de famille* during the day and
an ordinary table cloth for dinner. If kept folded in
a press it will last for a month spotlessly clean, provided that people are careful and that they use knife
rests, table mats, decanter stands; dish covers, when
taken off the dishes, should be placed on a china
dish or tray specially meant for them and put ready
on the table.

Paper napkins
People who are progressive will hardly object to paper napkins. Some are harsh with ugly coloured borders, but you can have quite plain soft white paper napkins, delightful in use.

Paper pocket handkerchiefs
For travelling, paper pocket handkerchiefs are ideal; they are as soft as silk. For great occasions use a lace handkerchief which you can wash yourself. When wet, spread it smooth on a marble slab; after drying in that way it comes out with exactly the right slight stiffness needed. When away from marble halls, spread it on a pane of glass.

To wash at home is hard work, but in life hard things must be faced.

Wash at home
If things are not allowed to become too soiled, and
are well sorted, if you rise earlier than usual, for
one morning in the fortnight, and on that day your
husband comes back early from work to act sloppy
and 'turn for you' it may not be so dreadful.

Outside help
Outside help could be procured; say a woman to
come in every other week for a day to assist. Where
only grown-ups form the family, washing once a
month should suffice; enough clothes could be possessed to last out, all towels, pillow cases could be
mended beforehand, plenty of soap-jelly provided,
the dinner cooked beforehand and visitors kept at
bay. It would soon be done and the satisfaction that
all had been kept sweet and clean would be great
indeed.

washing once
a month

Soap-suds

Many people object to the smell of soap-suds pervading a house and to damp linen being about the kitchen. Wet objects need not be in the way if you have a little backyard or a garden, and if not, a clothes airer and dryer high up in the kitchen, where the heat is greatest, can be used; any carpenter can make you one. If clothes are well wrung and mangled they dry very quickly, and the more the water is pressed out of them the less they are liable to shrinkage.

Iron shoes

Ironing is now facilitated by irons wearing shoes in almost human fashion; thus no cleaning of the iron is necessary and no soiling of clothes occurs.

MENDING

Clothes need regular mending and the better that is done the less frequently it needs to be done; mending can be got through often while watching the dinner cooking, while talking to your husband in the evening, or during a friend's visit.

If a friend is a real friend she will have a thimble in her pocket and help you while she chats.

Patching and darning

To mend well one must have the necessary cottons and wools handy. Pieces belonging to the garments should be kept sorted in boxes so that no time is lost in matching them. If the holes are large they must be patched; if this occurs on woven garments they have to be darned. It is difficult to darn

Darner.

well if the hole is large, say on the elbow of a sleeve, or on a knee, or on a heel; but if you take a piece of coarse netting or canvas the size of the hole and baste it in position and then work your darning through the net or canvas, it makes a sort of fancy work and a very even darn.

Socks or stockings should always be darned on a wooden or metal egg, so as to have both hands free.

It is wise to examine the inside of all boots and shoes for often holes in hose are caused by nails or by rough inside edges of the footgear.

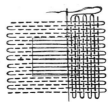

Buttonholes

Wherever you can, replace a button by a double buttonhole - as on underclothing - and thread a ribbon through both holes, you will be well advised to do so. On such things as towels, which have to hang up, work a good-sized buttonhole and hang it thereby on the hook; the buttonhole will last as long as the cloth, and there will be no necessity constantly to sew on tapes.

**Don'ts
and
Buts**

❧ *Don't*

Allow your hands to be stained

But

If dirty rub them with a piece of raw potato, or
with a lemon

❧ *Don't*

Allow linen which is not in use to remain long in
the same folds, or it will wear out at the fold

But

Change the fold

❧ *Don't*

Allow milk to turn sour

But

Use up the day's milk each evening for a pudding
however small, for next day

❧ *Don't*

Forget to put a basin of hot water in the oven when

you bake cakes

❧ *Don't*

Allow petroleum, ammonia, turpentine, or matches, within reach of children

But

Keep them locked up and high

❧ *Don't*

Allow hands that have touched the horse, the motor, or the boy's head to have access to your bread

But

Ask the baker to deliver bread cased in a paper bag

❧ *Don't*

Allow the rollers of the mangle to be pressed tight when damp, or they will crack in the centre

But

Always unscrew them and allow air to pass freely between them

The Servantless Household

❧ *Don't*
Allow pieces of bread to accumulate
But
Use them up for puddings or bake them and crush
them, and bottle the crumbs for future use

❧ *Don't*
Allow a kettle to get furred
But
Keep a marble in it

❧ *Don't*
Allow gas burners to be without ceiling shades
But
Have shades of glass or enamel

❧ *Don't*
Put much blacking on boots, it cracks them
But
Use much light elbow-grease

&ret; *Don't*
Allow your butter to turn soft
But
Place it under an inverted flower pot which has
been thoroughly wetted and butter will keep firm
in the hottest weather

&ret; *Don't*
Forget to have a 'baby' sweeper in each of your
principal rooms stowed in a corner, so as instantly
to sweep up any mud, dust, crumbs, &c. They cost
a couple of shillings each and make nice toys

&ret; *Don't*
Put salt to fish or roast meat till it is nearly cooked
or it will get hard in the cooking

&ret; *Don't*
Put anything very hot, such as a pie-dish fresh from
the oven, on a cold stone or slab or it will crack

73

But
Place a mat or paper underneath

❧ *Don't*
Put clothes to dry on the back of a chair, as the damp and heat will loosen the back of the chair
❧ *Don't*
Put down a broom with the bristles on the floor
But
Always put it with the bristles upwards or hang it up
❧ *Don't*
Put the paper flat in a grate
But
Make it into loose balls
❧ *Don't*
Put a dish cover on the table cloth or floor, it will wet or grease it

But
Keep a china tray or dish on the table to receive
dish covers

❧ *Don't*
Put cake and biscuits in the same tin, as one will
spoil the other
But
Put them in separate tins

❧ *Don't*
Throw away banana peel
But
Clean brown boots with the inside of the peel

❧ *Don't*
Throw away the stones of dates
But
Plant them in pots and raise palms

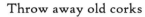 *Don't*
Throw away old corks
But
Save them, soak them in paraffin and use as a fire reviver

Don't
Throw any orange peel
But
Dry it and use it as a fire reviver

Don't
Throw away cake crumbs
But
Bottle them to sprinkle over puddings

Don't
Throw away cream that has been whipped too long
But
Go on whipping, make it into butter and begin anew

❧ *Don't*
Throw away old incandescent gas mantles
But
Crush them into powder and use for cleaning plate
❧ *Don't*
Throw away an egg because it has cooked too much
But
Hold it under the cold water tap and it will soften
from sheer fright

❧ *Don't*
Throw away an egg because it is not cooked enough
But
Replace the piece of shell in position and cover the
join with salt and cook again to taste
❧ *Don't*
Throw away small pieces of cooked vegetables
But

Cook them au gratin, either mixed up or singly

❧ *Don't*

Throw away odd pieces of soap

But

Make soap jelly of them by placing them in a jar and covering with boiling water

❧ *Don't*

Throw away a mackintosh or umbrella because it is torn

But

Patch it with a piece of the same coloured stuff and apply this on the wrong side by means of seccotine.

❧ *Don't*

Throw away a loaf of bread because it is too stale

But

Dip it in milk, or milk and water, and bake it in the

oven till the outside is crisp

🌸 *Don't*

Throw away wooden skewers.

But

Wash them and use them for cleaning out corners

🌸 *Don't*

Admit mice or flies to your house

But

Keep them away by covering everything

> *Remember one single crumb will attract a fly*

 🌸 *Don't*

Close a gas oven door after baking

But

Leave it open for a while to allow moisture to escape and to prevent rust forming

❧ *Don't*
Bang an oven door
But
Shut it gently

❧ *Don't*
Be downhearted if you cannot afford to buy a knife-cleaning machine
But
Stick your knives simply in the earth; they will clean themselves and if you have no garden, a flowerpot of earth will do

❧ *Don't*
Be sad if your crockery has been much broken
But
Mend it

❧ *Don't*
Be without a bottle of lime-water and linseed oil

on the kitchen shelf
But
If you have a burn or scald, shake the bottle and
apply instantly
❧ *Don't*
Buy house flannels
But
Keep old socks, open and stich them together, and
use them for floor cleaning
❧ *Don't*
Clean linoleum, or cork carpet with water
But
Clean it with turpentine
❧ *Don't*
Clean white wood tables, boards &c with hot water
But
Clean with cold water and sand

❧ *Don't*
Cook with the ordinary chocolate
But
Make chocolate with cocoa, flavour with sugar and
vanilla to taste
❧ *Don't*
Dry a chamois leather before the fire
But
Dry it in a draught
❧ *Don't*
Fill a bed-warmer half full, or it will cool quickly
But
Fill it to the brim
❧ *Don't*
Keep opening the oven door when you bake
But
Wait patiently till the time is up

❧ *Don't*
Give teacups, saucers and plates for afternoon tea
But
Put the cup on the plate (without the saucer) to receive cake and to avoid handling a third article

❧ *Don't*
Leave the fire without a safety guard
❧ *Don't*
Wash anything that has touched fish with other things
❧ *Don't*
Iron out thin handkerchiefs or laces
But
Spread them wet on a flat surface of marble and wait till they are dry

> *You will be surprised and delighted at the result*

❧ *Don't*
Keep lemons in the paper bag in which they come
But
Set each lemon on the egg-tray like an egg
❧ *Don't*
Let cheese turn stale
But
Wrap it in a cloth soaked in vinegar to keep moist
❧ *Don't*
Leave soup in the stewpan over night
But
Pour it out in a basin

❧ *Don't*
Let cake turn stale
But
Always keep a fresh apple in the tin and the cake
will keep moist

❧ *Don't*

Peel potatoes; they cook better, eat better and go further if boiled in their skins

But

Peel before sending to table if necessary

❧ *Don't*

Let your vegetables lie about

But

Keep them in the different compartments of a vegetable rack

❧ *Don't*

Run into the kitchen before you can receive goods

But

Have in your lobby two china dishes and a pretty large basket on and in which to receive goods

❧ *Don't*

Open an umbrella to drying or it will split

But
Close it and put it handle downwards in a pail
❧ *Don't*
Pull off the wax from your finger if hot sealing wax has fallen on it
But
Leave the wax on for a time and no blister will rise
❧ *Don't*
Pull curtains with the hand
But
Have all curtains on pulley rods and pull cords only
❧ *Don't*
Read too many cookery or house-keeping books, or your thoughts will get muddled; there are so many different ways of doing things
❧ *Don't*
Rub clothes which are very muddy

But
Clean them with a piece of raw potato
❧ *Don't*
Scrape off mud from clothes or boots with a knife
But
Brush off with the edge of a penny, a bad penny
will do quite well for the purpose
❧ *Don't*
Send clothes to the wash if they are stained

But
Take out stains first: tea, coffee, ink and wine with
glycerine; grease with benzine
❧ *Don't*
Send your clock to the clockmaker because it has
stopped
But
Soak a piece of cotton-wool in paraffin and put it

in the clock case for a week. It will clean the clock from all dust through the fumes

❧ Don't

Send your knives to the manufacturer because the ivory handles have been made yellow

But

Rub the handles with turpentine

❧ Don't

Send clothes to the laundry without keeping a duplicate list

But

Keep a note book with a sheet of carbon paper

❧ Don't

Speak while you eat fish

But

If you happen to swallow a bone, at once drink lemon juice or vinegar, or any acid which will dissolve the fish bone

❧ *Don't*

Spend money on vanilla essence for flavouring

But

Keep a pod of vanilla in a well closed jar of soft sugar: the sugar will thus obtain the proper flavour

❧ *Don't*

Spend money on buying table salt

But

Crush ordinary salt, bake it in the oven, put it in a tin and add a teaspoon of cornflour

❧ *Don't*

Stick a fork into meat, to see if it is cooked

But

Use the back of a spoon or turn it with steak tongs

❧ *Don't*

Stir rice with a fork or spoon, or it will get pulpy

But
Shake the rice
❧ *Don't*
Touch a door with the hand and fingermark it
But
Take it by the handle only
❧ *Don't*
Trip over mats that curl up
But
Sew strong webbing to the edges
❧ *Don't*

Try to whip eggs in a hot kitchen
But
Allow them to cool in a basin on a stone floor or in
a draught, and they will whip up easily
❧ *Don't*
Use milk when making an omelette

But
Use water, and be sure to beat the white and yolks
of the eggs together

🌿 *Don't*
Use a knife that has peeled onions for other things
But
Put it in the earth to remove the odour

🌿 *Don't*
Use cruets of silver if you are busy
But
Have china or glass ones

🌿 *Don't*
Use the first water which has been boiled in a new
kettle
But
Throw it away

❧ *Don't*
Use elaborate trays
But
If possible, let them all be tiled or of porcelain. If you already possess an elaborate tray, cover it with a sheet of glass made to fit

❧ *Don't*
Wash a mincing-machine the moment you have done with it
But
Pass dry bread-crumbs through it before washing

❧ *Don't*
Wash jugs, bowls, cups or glasses which have contained milk till you have rinsed them free of all milk by means of cold water

❧ *Don't*
Wash a chamois leather in hot water
But
Wash it in lukewarm water with ammonia

Always have in your hall a boot mop, a box of
matches, a lantern, a cover for a bicycle in case
of rain, a slipper box, a box with pennies for
unstamped letters

Shoe Mop.

KITCHEN COSMETICS
BEAUTY FROM YOUR PANTRY
How to have a smooth clear complexion -
and other potions and preparations for
natural beauty.
Original ingredients from yesterday's
kitchens.

APPEARANCES
HOW TO KEEP THEM UP
ON A LIMITED INCOME
Use the housekeeping money wisely, train
the cook well, how to shop, how to plan a
modest dinner party.